2nd Edition

SWEET OLD FASHIONED MEMORIES

Robert Piper

To order additional copies of this book, contact:
Xlibris
844-714-8691
www.Xlibris.com
Orders@Xlibris.com

ISBN: Softcover   978-1-6698-6334-2
        EBook   978-1-6698-6335-9

Print information available on the last page

Rev. date: 01/18/2023

This is all my poem ENJOY!!!!!!!!!!

"People"

People hikes things
That look good
People like things
Look good
People likes clothes
That look good
People likes food
That taste good
People likes flashy
Cars that look good
People likes
To do things
An enjoy
Things that they work
Hard for their money
To enjoy doing and satisfy them self
And making them
Feel good

"Water"

Guys drink a cold beer
To quench their thirst
But what goes down better
Nothing like a cold
"Drink of Water"

"Things"

Things that go together
Things like a woman and a man
Rich and poor
Good and bad
Rain and sun
Moon and the stars
Boy and dog
Birds and bee's
Thunder and lighting
Trees and grass
Night and day
Love and hate
Fat and Water

"Beautiful world"

The tress and the grass
All these thing surround
Us in this beautiful
Worldwide we are living

"God's love"

Enjoy the things
That god gave
Us life to help
Out our brotherman
Like your spouse
And to keep sharing and caring
Keep trying to help
Build a better man more
Beautiful world to live
In peace, love, harmony

"Just Mother Nature"

Feel the cool fresh air
Blowing through my hair
I even seen
Pretty blue sky
Turned gray
Suddenly rain drops sailing
Out of the sky
Just a few minutes
Ago I was enjoy sipping on
Cold glass of
Lemonade watching the sun
"I was feeling good"
Now its start to rain
I'm inside with my wife
Just enjoy mother nature

"Saying"

They say good thing comes
To those who wait
They even say patience
It's a virtue

"Just listen"

Some say this
And some may say
That but I'll say this
I'm glad that
I got life, good health
And gives thanks
To God who help
Me keep these
Things in places
Or in order at all the time

"Thanks"

Thanks for the
Time, we shared together
Thanks to all the thing you have given me
And we spent together

"Time just slips away"

They say breaking
Up is hard to do
Well, it depends on
The kind of situation
It could happen to
Now and there
Right in front of your eyes
And just can't believe that so much
Time has gone again
Right in front of my eyes

"A new everything"

It's a new day
It's a new dollar
Next thing you know
Is that you dog
Needs a new collar

"Passion"

Some like coffee hot
Some like it cold
One thing I know
Is love coming in
All styles and all kinds
Of fashion that's why
My love comes with
So much passion

"The truth"

For years and years
I am hearing the preachers
Saying the same thing
Over and over
They keep on saying that
They believers are people
Who is not sure?
Of what they are doing

"Just a fact"

Up and down
Even when
That makes the world
Go round
Two to tangle

"Enjoying nature"

Guess what makes me
Feel good all the time
I feel good that I have
Life I feel good
That I feel good I can pray
I feel good that I can
Go outside sit when
At a tree and enjoy
The breeze blowing
The birds flying
The birds singing
All these things that help
Me to enjoy
Nature is a lot better

"Just write"

Some time I stop
And study how to write
A poem it takes a lot
Of thinking a lot
Of Creativity
Finds ways to express
Your feelings and putting on paper

"Just mine"

My mind is mine
What I do with my mind
It's my business
What you do with your mind
Its your business
Not mine

"Wakeup call"

I remember when I was growing up
Roster use to know the time every
Six o'clock in the morning
Well that has change
The roster is more
Modernize
The crow at six o'clock in the morning

Up and down

They say what goes
Up must come down
Well, I can tell you
This I don't know how
It gets up in the sky
But I can sure feel
I when it's sailing down
From the sky.

"Just free"

Just know dogs communicate
With each other
Just like human beings
Now check this out
Even though a bird
Can't talk like me
They have wings
An can fly in the sky
So fast so high and so free

"A bird"

Now watching a bird
Sitting on a branch by itself
In a tree
It shows so much peace
And tranquility just sitting
On a branch in a tree
Just enjoying the cool breeze

"Just fly"

Just watching the birds
Flying around the sky
No sign, no stop light, no intersection
No school crossing guard
Nothing their way
To stop them
Flying in the pretty beautiful
Blue sky

"Niko Niko"

Niko niko where did you go
Niko was sparrow that landed
On my window silly everyday
When moving forward
The windowsill niko
Just fly away when I looked
Out the window is said niko niko
Where did you go

"All about the children"

Put a spark and bright up
Our children education
Put more books on the shelf
Teach the children to write their
Own books to put on the market
Teach the ones who willing
To learn more

"Sweet old fashion"

Sometimes I lay in bed, and I start
To study about my life
Today is a day I am laying under
The tree is the same date when
We said Goodbye
I tried so hard to forget but just could not
I went over the good times
And the bad times for such a long time
I remember playing with my kids
Taking them to movies, kids, park
The thing we did together
All the precious times we shared together
I just couldn't forget

"Just a special lady"

This lady is so special
To me she just doesn't know how much she
Gives me so much energy
I remember when she asks me to break down
A brick wall with a sledgehammer
I started do it right away
I got so much energy
That I broke the wall down so fast
Things like this happen
When you have special
Lady right by your side

"Bravo"

My name is Bravo
And I stand four feet
Four inches tall
And everyone says
In close to dawn
And right next to the stupid
Very close to being a fool
And I just can't get nothing right
I trained at home
And he ran dead last
Going to fight a chicken
And he drops right
Before the fight
Know you know I
Just can't get nothing

"God made the world"

Some say it's good
Some say it's bad
And some say God
Came in mysterious ways

"Just living"

She so beautiful
And her eyes
Glitter like gold
When I look in her eyes
She hypnotizes me
All the time
That I said yes so
Many time that I almost lost
Track that when I was supposed to
Say I do I did
Now she's my wife
Hypnotize for life

"Jesus is coming"

Watching this lady
So beautiful
So, universe
So, one of a kind
Say things like
This last to blow
Your mind
She said Jesus is vomming
Yes, Jesus is coming
But neither one
Of us knows
When he'll be here
But Jesus is coming
That's a fact

"Good of Miss Johnson"

Good morning, Miss Johnson
Dressed in blue
And I like your
Brand new hair
Do what else is brand new
Miss Johnson
Oh, it's a brand new
beautiful day in Paradise

"Always by your side"

I called a loved one
This morning and I
Say to her
I dream of you
All last night
Even you're so far away
I felt you right next
To my side
I know that you still
Care you still share
All these things
Brings you so close
Like you're here with
Me all the time

Printed in the United States
by Baker & Taylor Publisher Services